SILENT NO MORE

Sister Anne Sophie

SILENT NO MORE

Sister Anne Sophie

Queenship

PUBLISHING COMPANY
P.O. Box 220 • Goleta, CA 93116
(800) 647-9882 • (805) 692-0043 • Fax: (805) 967-5133

Published by:
    Queenship Publishing
    P.O. Box 220
    Goleta, CA 93116
    (800) 647-9882 • (805) 692-0043 • Fax: (805) 967-5133
    www.queenship.org

Printed in the United States of America

ISBN: 1-57918-269-0

DEDICATED TO ALL THE BABIES,
ESPECIALLY MY OWN LITTLE ONE
WHO WAS MURDERED BY
FORCED ABORTION

✝
Foreword

When the Son of God became man and entered our human experience, he drank fully the cup of our suffering. Through the mystery of the Cross he enabled each of us, in our hurt, to find healing and see through our own suffering a sharing in his work. The Gospels recount many stories of healing, but who will ever know the personal stories hidden behind these encounters with Jesus? One such story is the woman who suffered a deep personal injury for many years, seeking in vain for a cure (Mk 5:21-43). After fruitlessly searching for 12 years, her suffering and shame deeper than ever, she meets the Lord Jesus. With profound courage and faith, she reaches out to touch his garment from behind, finding herself face-to-face with him in public. Though none around her knew her story – and to the apostles she seemed just another anonymous face in the crowd – Jesus immediately knew her and knew her personally. In Him, this woman found the one who could see to the depth of her soul, understand her, and provide the compassion that would heal her and make her one of His followers.

By the time the Gospels were being written, everyone had come to know something of the background of this remarkable woman of faith, how she had struggled, how she had suffered, how she came to the Lord Jesus, how she found healing. But the Gospels also draw our attention to the connection between her miracle and that of the raising of Jairus' daughter (for twelve years she suffered, at twelve years the little girl died). The juxtaposition of these two miracles is not incidental. It shows how deep personal wounds rob innocence and destroy one's child-likeness. The healing of Jesus on the one hand cures an older woman of deep personal pain, and on the other hand brings to life the little girl. There is an image here of how healing for the adult woman is associated with the resurrection of childlike trust and joy, something that seemed to have "died" and been mourned, but in fact had "only been sleeping."

Sister Ann Sophie Meaney is one such woman who has suf-

fered grievous injury, that left bleeding wounds inside for many years. As a young girl, life robbed her of her childhood and inno- cence. As an adult, she discovered the healing presence of Jesus. She is a remarkable woman, and her life is a testimony to the grace of God and power of love. Her commitment to the neglected and dying, and her fearlessness in the face of human suffering are evi- dence of the supernatural presence of Jesus in her life and in her work with the Society of the Body of Christ. Her painful back- ground, in God's providence, has uniquely prepared her to be the Lord's instrument of love to all who experience suffering, espe- cially the terminally ill and mothers with crisis pregnancies.

Sr. Sophie is known around town for the distinctive blue habit she wears as a sign of her total consecration to Jesus. She has endearingly been called a "special-ops" nun, and that is indeed what she is! It is my prayer that her story will be an inspiration to other women who also live daily with unhealed injury. In good company with the holy women who followed Jesus, may her life story be a testimony to the healing love of Jesus, and the solicitude of Mary in bringing these disciples to Jesus.

Rev. Glen Mullan
Chaplain for the Society of the Body of Christ

Silent No More!

A Journey of Abuse, Rape, Forced Abortion which led to Adoption, A Vocation & A New Society

✝

As I was kneeling during the consecration of the Mass, my head bowed, laid deeply in the palms of my hands, I leaned against the top of the back of the pew in front of me. My eyes closed and in deep meditation I heard as if for the first time a newborn baby crying. How many times have I heard a baby crying during Mass? Many, many times!

For some reason, I instantly connected with this baby if only for a few moments. The baby's cries went right through me! I immediately felt overwhelmed. I just wanted to cry, no! I wanted to weep! Never had I sensed or felt these feelings before! Feelings and thoughts of grievous detachment. Along with the pain of the crying there was a sense of the special love and urgency of the mother responding to the innocence and love that emanates from the child. In total dependency the baby seeks maternal protection. Quite possibly the love between child and mother and mother and child is the purest love we know on earth, in its highest form the love between Mother Mary and Baby Jesus!

Why would a baby's cries at Mass all of a sudden affect me in such an overwhelming way? Because I was beginning to remember what years ago I had suppressed, and about which now I am able to write to give an account of this important part of my life. I want to share it with you, so that the tears in your eyes and the tears in your heart may not be of despair but of hope.

As a baby I was baptized a Catholic, for which I am very grateful. My birth mother was a first generation immigrant from the Azores Islands of Portugal. Because she was sick mentally and emotionally and thus very abusive as a parent, my childhood was difficult. Her physical, verbal and emotional abuse still haunts me. But I have managed to heal from it all slowly, through time and especially through the grace from God! He took me by the hand and led me into His heart where I love to repose and feel His peace.

I had two birth brothers, one about eight years older and one six years younger, and a birth sister who was about eleven years older.

Each of us was treated differently; the others didn't go through what I did and I don't know why. The neighborhood boys and my older birth brother sexually abused me when I was five years old. This went on for about a year. I was disturbed, confused and afraid. Finally, I told my birth parents. I remember distinctly my birth brother looking at me as if he wanted to do me harm! He called me a liar and I was punished. He wasn't questioned at all. At least the sexual abuse stopped.

My birth father was from the hills of Alabama and a non-Catholic who had converted to the faith. He was a quiet man but would blow up suddenly at the verbal abuse he got from my birth mother. Later, I learned that he was an adulterer and had several affairs during most of their married life. As I remember, when completely unglued he would get violent, many times turning over the kitchen table with the food flying through the air then he would enter into a physical fight with my birth mother. Everyone would scatter but, on occasion, small as I was, I would try to get between them to somehow make it all stop. I would be thrown to the side of the room. They finally divorced years later. He remarried, moved to another state, left the Church and died without the Sacraments. I found it odd that I hardly felt or showed any emotion.

Through all the trials, my greatest consolation was going to a

Catholic school. What a blessing! Once in a while one of the nuns would take me under her wing for the time she was my teacher. In first grade the nun was so kind to me that even to this day I have a fond memory of her. I was given speech therapy, as I was not able to talk like the other children.

I found great comfort in going into the church as often as I could during recess or before school started. In those days no one seemed to ever question parents' authority. My frequent tardiness was due to the physical and verbal abuse in the mornings while trying to get ready for school. Many mornings I left the house without eating. I remember trying to eat quickly some cut bananas with milk and sugar while crying before leaving for school and crying all the way while walking to school more days than not. I was in my own unhappy world.

One morning, I arrived at school very late; even so, I longed to go into the church, as I was so upset. I walked in and realized no one was there. Walking down the main aisle I stopped at the Blessed Mother statue, where there were beautiful lights from the many candles lit. It was so warm there and the Blessed Mother statue seemed so magnificent! I was in first grade and always felt very sad. I slowly approached the statue and it seemed as if the Blessed Mother were reaching for my hand! I placed my little hand in hers and looked up deep into her eyes, as she seemed to look down deep into mine.

As my tears flowed down my cheeks, I cried to her and asked her, "Blessed Mother will you be my mother?" I waited for a response but of course I heard none. Yet deep within my heart as I closed my eyes tightly I felt her response saying, "Yes, I will be your mother." That gave me great peace and consolation. Throughout my life I would feel her presence. She would be instrumental in bringing me close to her Son and eventually helping me to offer my life in service to Him.

It's amazing how one copes with traumatic experiences. How a little child just automatically tries to survive not even realizing how bad things really are. I remember continually reaching out for love no matter how much love as I knew it hurt. Above all else it is love that surpasses anything this world has to offer. God is love and there is no comprehending a world that tries to manipulate love.

Through more years of a trying journey I was about twelve or thirteen, again my dates are hard to remember, I was riding my bike to go get some cigarettes. Yes, I had begun smoking in seventh or eighth grade. I made many mistakes especially during those years.

I was lured and forced into a car driven by a complete stranger. I couldn't get out, as the car was a type that the door locks were hidden and I looked and looked but never could find the lock. The car sped off immediately. The man was probably around thirty-five years old and had a crew cut with blonde hair. His eyes were blue. I remember distinctly how looking into his eyes was like looking into a wall of hatred and evil. I couldn't reach him through his eyes. It was difficult to even try. I was terrified and asked him "Please drop me off here, please let me out!"

The more I pleaded with him, the angrier he looked. He didn't say a word as he drove onto the freeway. He seemed to know exactly where he was going. My heart felt as if it was in the pit of my stomach. I knew I was in trouble. I was so scared. He took the airport exit and went along the feeder road where they had big lots of parked rental cars. There must have been hundreds of them. He drove into one lot and backed the car into the parked cars area. He made sure when he backed up that he was just a few inches away from the other car on my side. In fact all the cars were parked that way.

I was silent and terrified. He turned off the engine and grabbed me by my hair in one hand and forced my head into his lap with his other hand under my neck and chin area. He said, "Look baby, it only takes five seconds to break your neck!"

I began to cry profusely. I thought I was going to die. I looked as deeply as I could into his eyes to try to reach him. There was a long silence, during which my life flashed in front of me interiorly. I even saw newspaper articles of a young girl's body found with her head detached from her body. There had been girls' bodies found in the same area. They were found right over the fence, which ran a long ways behind all the rental car parking lots. Beyond the fence there was the ocean. The silence felt like an eternity, but only seconds had actually passed.

He warned me "I will kill you if you scream or fight me!" He then raised my head and allowed me to sit up. I looked quickly out towards the front of the lot where I saw cars going by on the access road that led to all the lots and other nearby buildings. I even saw police cars from time to time go right by. I kept thinking, "If only they would come inside the lot!" But no one ever did.

Who would help me? What did I have to hang onto? Who would come and rescue me? I had one chance to survive. I felt God in the midst of it all. I intuitively knew that I would have to go along with whatever and try not to scream out or make this guy angrier than he already was. He was a sick man. He kept talking about his wife and daughter who supposedly went off a cliff in their car somewhere in New York. He kept talking over and over and over again about it almost as if he was trying to justify what he was about to do to me. That's all I knew.

Many things ran through my mind. Somehow I would survive. God would protect me, even if it meant I would have to endure the unspeakable. He stopped talking and forced me into the back of this station wagon that was already set up where the back section was flat. I began to shut down inside. I became frozen in time. I tried to block out the blows, the pain, the sexual acts, the taunting and the fear of being killed. I was in another world. I was able to turn off many emotions trying to ignore what was happening to me for at least some of the time.

All of a sudden he stopped what he was doing. He peered through the front window. He said, " Don't say a word! Be completely silent! I will kill you if you make a sound!"

What he saw was three teenage boys who had come into the lot evidently to strip some automobiles. They hadn't seen us in the car. This gave me time to think and pray. "How can I get out of this alive?" I thought. "God please help me!"

I really believe the Holy Spirit was placing some ideas in my mind as I thought that perhaps I could pretend to this man that I somehow all of a sudden had feelings for him. After all, if what he said was the truth about his wife and child, then he needs to feel love. As sick and horrible as he is, as repulsive the idea was, it was the only thing that really came to mind and quite possibly my only chance of surviving! Maybe as sick as he is, maybe it would work! I thought quite possibly I would die trying.

I remember being in pain and trying to ignore those feelings concentrating on what words to use. I was very worried about triggering his anger. I knew and could sense that my time was running out. I feared more than anything else what way he would kill me. All of a sudden I began to talk softly to him. I said something like "I know this will sound weird but I really am beginning to have feelings for you. I never have felt these feelings before. I think I am falling in love with you."

He looked at me and didn't say a word. I was relieved some because what I said didn't seem to anger him, but I wasn't sure how else I could try to convince him of my fake feelings. It was all a matter of survival. He kept watching the teenage boys. He said, "Don't say a word or I will kill you!"

Finally, after what seemed an eternity, the boys walked through the lot and left. I told the man that if he would let me go, I would meet him the next day. That way no one would know anything had happened, that I wouldn't talk to anyone about it and I would meet him at 8:30 in the morning at the same place where he had taken me. I would say about ten minutes or so passed in silence and he turned on the car and not a word was said as he drove.

He drove out of the airport area onto the freeway back to where my bike was still lying where it fell on the side of the street. I could hardly breathe from being so scared and upset. He pulled the car over to the side of the street and said "You be here at 8:30 tomorrow morning or I will find you and kill you" "Don't talk to anyone about this. You be here!"

He unlocked the door. I left the car, thanked God and got on my bike and rode as I never had before, up the steep streets as if the bike were motorized. Fast and faster I rode. I got home and walked through the front door of the house where my birth mother had begun screaming at me, grabbing me by the hair. I don't remember what she said. You see I was still in another world, as if frozen emotionally, mentally and physically in time.

I ran straight into the bathroom where I took several showers. I didn't sleep at all that night. I never told anyone what happened. I never saw that horrible man again. I remained scared for a long time. I never reported it. Somehow, I just couldn't bring myself to talk about it.

I also remember hearing about other girls who had been raped and murdered, some even decapitated. I just knew it must have been the same man, but I couldn't bring myself to go to the authorities. That silence has always been hard to live with.

Some time had passed and things at home became much worse. There was no peace; everything was very tense, showing a total lack of love, interest, communication, nurturing and supervision. More than ever before, any attention from my birth mother was through verbal and physical abuse. My birth father was hardly ever home. I was rightfully kicked out of the best school I could have attended. I just couldn't concentrate on schoolwork. It seemed impossible to even try.

I got to the point that I withdrew from the world and ran away several times. The trouble I got into from time to time caused much difficulty for others and myself. I still feel guilty over it to this day. Some of my so-called friends were deceiving me and had done some things that I was unaware of, and I even got into trouble because of association with these people. I became more and more withdrawn. One day I walked into the nurse's office at the public school I was then attending and told the nurse who actually lived across the street from our house that I couldn't take it anymore. She was very kind and seemed to understand completely as she as well as the other neighbors had been observing for a long time the behavior of my birth mother.

The nurse immediately called a doctor. I remained quietly waiting and open to any help I would receive. That was part of my problem. I was too quiet. The nurse drove me to see the doctor who was very kind and gentle. You might be asking the question, did I share with him about the rape? No, I never did. We spoke of my home life and the abuse. I had run away from home already a couple of times. I just couldn't handle the abuse anymore. I was getting into trouble in staying away from the house, hiding out so to speak. I never felt like I belonged in that family. It was all so very strange. Nothing seemed right at home. I had always felt estranged and always on my own. I was very lonely.

The doctor told me I needed a vacation, that I needed to be away from my birth parents. I was placed in a neuro-psychiatric center for a few months. I did not have any visitors but a nun and a priest. If you have ever seen the movie "One Flew Over the Coo Coos Nest", this place made the movie look like an understatement! I had to re-sharpen my survival skills for this new adventure!

There were men and women of all ages there. Being an adolescent, I was the youngest person there. They had all types of problems. Some were there for shock therapy, (thank God I didn't have that!). Some were in there for drug addictions like heroin; some were in there for exposing themselves, etc. I was drawn to and felt sorry for an ex-nun who was in a deep depression and was suicidal. I was always looking for her and talking with her. She was always very pleasant and kind to me. I could see in her facial expressions how sad she was and how difficult it was for her to cope with life.

I witnessed several suicide attempts from different patients, from overdosing on medications to breaking glass and cutting wrists, to my roommate jumping off the third story roof. It was really a dangerous place to be, especially for an adolescent. There was even an elderly man who probably was about seventy something; somehow he had gotten hold of a switchblade knife! As I was watching television one night in the recreation room he approached me and opened the knife up against my forehead! He didn't cut me because I managed to get away and hide for a short time while the staff tried to find him and take the knife from him.

Yes, that place was quite an experience in itself. God protected me through this as well. But absolutely nothing in my life was making any sense. No one told me what was happening or why I was going through any of it.

My doctor recommended foster care and I became a ward of the State. During the legal formalities I was placed in a juvenile hall facility. In a court proceeding I witnessed the presiding judge asking my birth mother if she realized that she was relinquishing all legal rights to me as her child. She said yes with no hesitation or feeling. The judge likewise asked my birth father the same question. He said he agreed with whatever his wife wanted. It was then official and I was sent back to a private cell where I waited until I was sent away to a foster home, a hundred and fifty miles away to a little town in the San Joaquin Valley.

I never missed my birth family. I don't remember even thinking about them. I guess I was just trying to go on with my life, trying to find my way, feeling very lonely but trusting God. The doctor had told me before I left that neuro-psychiatric center that my birth mother was the one that needed to be in there, not me! For some reason, that made me feel better.

The foster home was a disappointment to say the least. I was dropped off and when I entered the house, my new foster mother was drunk. She evidently was an alcoholic who preferred Napoleon Brandy. She drank a small bottle every day. The foster father was living in a local motel. They were in the middle of a divorce. The couple was supposedly given about $150.00 a month from the state to take care of me. He owned a motorcycle and radiator shop. He was a nice man.

She was very temperamental and I think she saw me as a live-in maid who cleaned up after her and her two children. I was given a cot to sleep on in the hallway.

The first night I was there, my foster mother had passed out drunk. It was about three in the morning by then and I struggled to take her to her bedroom so she could at least sleep on her bed, then I left her room and closed her door. As I walked down the hallway to my cot a tall man walked through the backdoor into the house. He walked over to me and asked if I was the foster kid. I said "yes". He introduced himself as the boarder who lived upstairs in the attic bedroom. He invited me upstairs to see where he lived, so

I went.

Once upstairs he closed his door and forced me down on his bed and even though I told him to get off and let me go, he would not, and he raped me. I immediately went into the same emotional and physical mode of shock, of turning myself off into a frozen-in-time existence as I had done when I had been raped and almost killed about two years before. I think this must be some sort of automatic protection system, one that my mind clicked into and thus my body followed. I also believe that this state of being helped me not to feel so much and suppressed my memory in an attempt to block out the pain. At least I was not beaten.

After what seemed a long time, I was finally let up off the bed. He warned me not to say a word to anyone and he would leave me alone. Otherwise, he would make sure I regretted it. I went downstairs and sat on my cot for hours until I saw sunlight rays coming through the top windows of the back door. It was a difficult time in my life and the days were long. I never told anyone what had happened until a few months had passed by. I realized I hadn't had my menstrual period and still I waited probably another month before I said anything, as I was so scared to tell anyone. My foster mother had a harsh temper.

But one day I tried to talk with her before she got too drunk and I told her what had happened. The next day she whisked me off to a doctor where she had him give me a shot that would bring my period on if I weren't pregnant. All the way home from the doctors office, she was angry over the fact that the shot had cost $10.00. Nothing else was said.

A few days later I was taken once more to the doctor where I waited after a blood test was taken. I was pregnant. She was furious and took me home. I was four months pregnant! She confronted the boarder and all I know is that he left town the next day. I actually saw him driving down the freeway in the fast lane leaving town! To this day he has no idea if he has a child in this world or not. I don't think he cared.

My probation officer, who supposedly looked after me while I was a ward of the State, was finally informed. She never came to visit me. She told my foster mother that no ward of the State was allowed to have a baby and that an abortion had been set up with some doctor that I had never seen in another town nearby.

In the meantime, I was given many concoctions to drink and scalding hot baths to sit in at home. No one talked with me about the fact that I was carrying a little baby who was by then in the fifth or sixth month, kicking in my womb. Not the doctor, probation officer, school counselor, foster parents, not anyone talked with me about what was happening or what an abortion really meant or the fact that I had been raped. I was treated as though I was promiscuous.

My mind seemed to be as if in deep thought all the time. Without words just diverse feelings of the severity of what was happening to me. No one addressed any of these things. I did not understand why decisions were being made without discussion with me.

The State-scheduled abortion was cancelled by the doctor who had an emergency the morning I was to be taken in for it. I felt so relieved! The delay was building more and more stress and tension in the house, and my foster mother had lost rental income. She was one-day drunk and screaming at me, calling me many horrible names and complaining about how much this pregnancy has cost her.

I became very depressed and decided to run away and there I was the next day on the side of the interstate highway, hitchhiking. My foster father happened to be driving past, saw me and stopped to pick me up. He was kind and apologized for everything that had happened to me. I began to cry quietly as I looked out the side window.

It was all so overwhelming. He dropped me off at the house and there I found my foster mother listening to music and completely drunk again.

I don't know why I did this because I really had no intention of hurting myself but I went upstairs with a razor blade I had found in the bathroom and I cut my left wrist. I did not intentionally want to really cut my wrist but I had no idea how a razor blade worked.

I found out quickly! It was so sharp that blood came squirting out fast like a fountain. I became sick right away and scared to death from having done it! (When I look back now I realize how fragile I was.)

I ran downstairs, and nothing I tried stopped the bleeding so I called my foster father, and he took me to the hospital where I was stitched up. That day, I received a special delivery letter from a dear Sister of Mercy nun, Sr. Marie Eloise. She was always following me by keeping track of where I was through the foster homes where I was placed. Her letter couldn't have come at a better time. I kept that letter for many years as it meant so much to me. She was the only one that tried to save my baby from being aborted! When she found out I was pregnant, I guess she knew everyone was deciding that I would have an abortion and to no avail tried to be an advocate to stop it from happening. No one ever said the word ADOPTION. I NEVER remember ever hearing that beautiful word!

Her letter was consoling and told me to be strong and not have an abortion. At the same time, her letter brought more conviction in my heart NOT to let anything happen to the baby. But I was totally alone with my conviction, and no one shared it except for St. Marie Eloise and she was far away.

For several years I hadn't known that the State had requested my biological parents to pay for the abortion. They did pay the money and even provided the doctor! In fact, I was returned to the juvenile facility back home. My birth father picked me up and drove me to the hospital where I was given a shot and prepared for surgery. It seemed like I was whisked off in such a hurry with no words in the car on the way to the hospital.

Although I cried hysterically, no one seemed to care. I was six and a half months pregnant by then. The baby was murdered by abortion.

I remember bleeding profusely for about a week and a half afterwards. I think I was fifteen when the abortion was done, I'm not sure. I was informed that people were told I had my tonsils removed!

The State took me to see the old doctor who killed my baby as a follow-up appointment. The only thing I remember asking him was if the baby was a girl or a boy. He said he couldn't tell because the baby was in a million pieces!

I had been placed in a total of five foster homes. None was appropriate as each one had major problems. Yet the best one was the last home I was placed in and it was a single parent, who brought me to Texas. Needless to say I never missed California! My last foster mother was a very good woman who one day died of cancer in my arms.

In the many years after the abortion, it took several more years to put all the pieces together. The abortion has always been on my mind and in my heart. The thoughts of it are much clearer now than before. It is hard to know if I will ever completely remember all the details. What matters the most is that God allowed it all to happen for a reason, and He has worked through the pain and suffering to bring healing, grace and peace.

The fact remains that my birth parents had absolutely no remorse for what they did, even years afterwards. That entire family is pro-choice and thinks that I am completely crazy for being against abortion. It will always be unacceptable that they have no remorse for the killing of my baby. Is there life after abortion? THERE IS ETERNAL LIFE! I wish everyone would realize we must live eternally with the decisions we make in this world.

Eventually God would lead me to become active in the pro-life cause here, peacefully rescuing babies through prayerful sit-ins. I was arrested on Good Friday one year while at the local abortion killing center in town. For my punishment the judge gave me one hundred community service hours at Birthright! I was really surprised to receive that sentence!

So, in obedience to the judge, there I was walking into Birthright not realizing that I was about to meet my future mother that God had chosen to adopt me! I guess God doesn't have an age limit in these matters! The thought never entered my mind!

She whom I met was an unbelievably dedicated, unselfish, all giving, overworked, loving French woman who was warm in wel-coming me in and asked me to sit down. She had founded the local Birthright several years before. I proceeded to explain why I was there and told her what had happened with the judge in my sen-tencing, and before I knew it I began to share with her a little about my own abortion. What she didn't realize is that it was the first time in all those years that had gone by that I talked about it.

But even then, I wasn't quite clear in how everything had hap-pened with the abortion in relation to the responsibility of my birth parents etc. Why were they involved when I had become a ward of the State? I guess I will never know. One thing for sure is that they had a choice to do it or not. They chose wrong. They chose death. They chose mortal sin. They had killed their own grandchild.

Going to see my adoptive mother to be for the first time was like opening up the lid of Pandora's box! In time, I began to re-member more and more. It really isn't until the last few years that somehow the most important pieces have come together. Now, I am able to accept what has happened and live my life, which has been transformed in every way! It has been transformed by the healing power of love!

In these days I strive to live my life serving God in ministering to others from conception to natural death. In this world it is the only existence for me that makes any sense, that is cherishing life and realizing how important each life truly is. The potential for each soul is the life-giving fact that the source for its life is God and each soul, each life should be protected at all costs.

As far as my birth parents are concerned I have placed them in God's hands and His forgiveness. Through His grace, His forgive-ness can I forgive, knowing that in the end we will all be judged by LOVE.

The good news is that my parents eventually adopted me in my adult years! Everyone thought it would be a great healing experi-ence for me and it has been. My father also has been very involved in the pro-life efforts here and even was incarcerated in Austin for prayerfully rescuing at an abortion-killing center. My family and I are very proud of Dad for that! I believe God's will was that this wonderful family would adopt me. But in order for that to happen the idea had to come first from God and He had to reveal it to us!

My mother and I shared a very deep grace-filled spiritual experience that Our lady of Guadalupe indeed had a plan that was about to be revealed! In order for this to happen, the both of us would be led to another country—to her shrine at the Basilica in Mexico City. It would be a life changing special pilgrimage for the both of us!

For years mother had not been able to do many things she used to because of severe orthopedic, nerve and muscular problems. She couldn't even turn her head or bend down to tie her shoes! After my parents invited me to come and live with them during the first years, this pilgrimage trip came up, and an answer to whether we were going or not had to be made.

So mother prayed to Our Lady of Guadalupe one night that if she wanted her to take me to her shrine in Mexico city, that she would need a healing in order to go and endure traveling in the bus, etc. The next morning mother awakened with elation and great surprise when she realized she was able to put her shoes on and had no more pain or neuralgia! She knew Our lady of Guadalupe had heard her prayer and she also knew that she was to take me and go on this pilgrimage! Many beautiful graces were felt for the both of us! It was an amazing pilgrimage as we became very close through the powerful intercession of Our Lady of Guadalupe! It was almost unbelievable, the whole experience.

I knew deep in my heart with childlike confidence that Our Lady was somehow preparing me by this pilgrimage for what God intended me to do in His name the rest of my life. I also felt that it was not to be an easy road but I just couldn't feel anything but pure joy! After arriving at the Basilica, I told mother that I could not approach Our Lady without coming to her by walking on my knees the entire outside length of the courtyard which led into the basilica. I wanted to bring her all the sick and especially the dying from my arms and heart into hers.

I began the special walk on my knees. I did not avoid any rocks or broken glass along the way. I think the stones were lava rock and after several feet, my knees were in excruciating pain and tears began to flow down my cheeks. I tried not to cry but ignored the pain and prayed for those Christ placed in my path to serve – all the sick and dying. With every motion forward, my eyes focused through the opened front door to the Basilica where I could see clearly the Tilma with the image of Our Lady of Guadalupe! I asked Our Lady as I gazed upon her image to give me the strength to continue my journey for those I was carrying to her in my heart to finish this walk on my knees to her.

As I approached the entrance steps, I realized that somewhere along the way my mother was following behind me on her knees too. What a woman! We met as we were coming up the stairs together and finished on our knees arm in arm. We were both crying as we entered the Basilica, our eyes fixed upon the image of Our Lady of Guadalupe.

One of the other pilgrims that was on our bus came over and asked mother a question, and she got up and walked off with him. I stayed as I was on my knees, focused on Our Lady's image on the Tilma. A Mexican woman, probably in her late sixties or early seventies, came up to me and looked down at me saying in perfect English "Our Lady wants you to pick a rose from her shrine!"

I turned to look for my mother, and within just a couple of seconds I turned back to say thank you to this woman, but she was gone and I couldn't find her. She had disappeared! I never saw her again. I had a hard time getting up off my knees and the pain was almost unbearable by now, but I made my way to Our Lady's shrine and picked a rose from the base of it. As I stood there contemplating the walk, the prayers along the way, my mother walking beside me on her knees, entering together to greet and honor Our Lady in her shrine and this request from Our Lady through this humble Mexican woman I realized that these were grace filled moments in time. The grace received from that day has never left my heart and soul!

I gave the rose I picked from the shrine to my mother who pressed it and framed it where she displays it in her dining room. For several days my mother was taking pieces of rocks and glass out of my knees. What graces we shared and still do from this unique experience which affects us to this day! We bonded as only a mother and a child could and for the first time in my life I felt that bond between a mother and child with her. It was the beginning of a healing process that I believe was the intention of the Blessed Mother. Prior to this pilgrimage I had been leading the fifteen-decade rosary at a main park in our city along the waters edge for over three years. Many of us who met there faithfully emerged from that prayerfulness to become active in different apostolates. I trusted the Blessed Mother to lead me not only closer to her Son but also wherever she desired to take me!

Mother and I returned home full of joy, as it was a life changing experience for both of us! One of the many fruits from the pilgrimage after a lot of prayer, mother and dad discussed the possibility of adoption with my siblings to be and the rest of the family. We believe the powerful intercession of Our Blessed Mother, led us to seek the spiritual direction of our then Bishop Rene H. Gracida. Receiving his blessing to go ahead with the adoption, my name was legally changed as well as my baptismal record.

Through this whole experience mother actually saved my life because we discovered that I had been a diabetic for several years and left untreated, needed insulin shots. You see, she is a retired medical doctor and my father is a Doctor of Philosophy. My siblings were welcoming and open in receiving me as their sister. Through the years we have become very close. My beloved brother Joseph is working for Human Life International and his wife, Marie, is like another sister. She teaches and is very active in the pro-life cause too.

My amazing sister, Mary is a consultant for an International firm and my brother-in-law, Ian, of whom I am very fond, and more like an actual brother, is a professor of Roman Archaeology at London University. They have three children, my nieces Isabelle, Claire and Emily, my godchild. Ian and Mary are very involved and active in the pro-life cause internationally, as are Joseph and Marie.

My sister Elizabeth is a wonderful teacher and gifted artist who lives in France with her husband Jean-Pierre, who is an engineer and talented wood worker. Their children are my nephew Santiago, niece little Helen, and precious new baby Francois! Yes, I have been truly blessed! There is already a happy ending to this story personally and still it's not over yet! God is so good and He continues to send me His love in special ways! The best is yet to come!

This is the process which led me to my vocation. For me the most important part of a vocation is being used for the salvation of souls! The compassion for human life from conception to natural death has always been a great gift deep within. This compassion is hard to see in this world.

I began to volunteer at Birthright, and God used me to help change the mind of women who were seeking abortions when I shared what I remembered of my own. I felt called and became a Eucharistic minister for the sick and dying. After training through a local Catholic hospital I began visiting these precious souls at their bedside and working closely with children who were dying of cancer and their families.

A dear friend, Sr. Nancy Johnson, helped me to see that indeed I did have a vocation to the religious life and to follow where God was leading me. She remains one of my closest confidants.

At one point I was seeing two persons for spiritual direction, a nun and a priest. Both were convinced that I was to be used in beginning a new religious community. They sensed this fire of love and compassion in my heart that God may have plans for me in serving others. I had absolutely no idea what they were talking about. I just kept working and visiting the sick, and one day in obedience to my priest-director, I went to seek spiritual direction from Bishop Joseph Galante, who had been at the Vatican from 1987 to 1992 in charge of the Congregation for Institutes of Consecrated Life and Societies of Apostolic Life.

I shared with him the vision of my heart. I spoke of the great need for spiritual support and direction to the sick, the elderly and the dying. There are so many not being served by the Church. I felt called to be used in the saving of babies and a great urgency to be used somehow in the saving of souls!

There are so many fallen away Catholics who are not being reached and are being lost. I knew deep inside that many could be reached through this ministry of love and compassion. After sharing all I could with Bishop Galante for about fifty minutes, he said "I would like you to go immediately to Bishop Gracida when you return home and share with him what you have told me."

After this important meeting, upon my return, I prayed intensely and wrote to Bishop Gracida all that was in my heart. Within a few weeks he wrote back that it was his intention to erect the Society of the Body of Christ as a Public Association of the Faithful with the objective being that it will someday include a religious institute! Imagine my surprise and elation! Imagine my parents' surprise and elation! We were definitely overwhelmed with joy!

I was given the privilege of making private promises of poverty, chastity, obedience and to defend all human life from conception to natural death. I received my distinctive garb and became a consecrated handmaid of the suffering Christ Our Lord on the feast of the Annunciation March 25, 1994 in the Corpus Christi Cathedral. Dear Bishop Gracida also formally erected the Society of the Body of Christ as a Public Association.

There have been many souls served through this ministry. Bishop Gracida retired in 1996, but we continue to give thanks and praise to God, for He continues to use us to do His will. We pray for holy vocations with great anticipation. It is, after all, a special call to serve Jesus in the unwanted babies of the womb, to serve Jesus in the sick, the elderly and the dying, in the confused and lost. One day I know God will send these holy vocations to service at the foot of the Cross. I refer to them as handmaids of the suffering Christ.

I am also an Oblate of the Congregation of St. John. When I was adopted, my mother being French, I automatically received my French roots! My great uncle Marie Dominic Philippe is the founder of the Congregation of St. John. When we first met, he outstretched his arms and said, "I welcome you my niece!"

I went into his warm arms of love, and he expressed to me that he felt the charism of the Society of the Body of Christ was the compassion of Mary at the foot of the Cross through St. John!

His words are etched in my heart and mind. For his words best describe our charism and thus our special connection to the Order of St. John. In my heart I know there are no coincidences with God. For me it is always His will. This is what I have come to desire most.

My spiritual director since 1992 has been Fr. Dominic Faure of the Congregation of St. John. He is a holy priest who now works with the dying in India. The Society of the Body of Christ currently has 96 Lay Associate members, 376 Suffering Members (those whom we serve and who offer their suffering for the glory of God) and one consecrated member, myself. Our ministry is centered in the Holy Eucharist; the Congregation of St. John provides monthly spiritual formation. Another special blessing has been our Chaplain of many years, Fr. Glen Mullan. He has stood by us, has encouraged and supported us all the way and is a dear friend.

Queenship Publishing has recently published *On The Front Lines,* a book I wrote which comprises true stories of the suffering embraced by Christ through our ministry. It is also available on CD. There is a new booklet called *Being Born into Eternal Life,* a spiritual guide for the dying which is very helpful for family and friends of the dying person which can be used at their bedside.

We are most excited to have just finished an important instrument of the Holy Spirit, a new CD called *On Our Way To Paradise.* It is our ministry on CD. It has prayers, songs, the full rosary, litanies of fear, the Blessed Mother, Saints and St. Joseph, psalms and spiritual direction from holy priests. This CD is a spiritual journey for the suffering and for daily preparation for eternal life. It is great for anyone at home, traveling in the car, the sick, the elderly and the dying. Many people have called us to say how inspirational it is. Finally, because of requests there is a music CD available called "All I Ask Is Love", which contains music I have written.

Who could have imagined His plans! God continues to do marvelous works, saving souls and lives through the Society of the Body of Christ. Babies' lives have been spared and born into this world.

One in particular was even adopted and we were used in finding a good Catholic home for the baby. My only regret is that I was unable to do that for my little baby. No one seemed to care about that little baby's life.

That is why even though I know now the truth about the past and the healing grace that can come only from God, I joined a nationwide organization called Silent No More Awareness. It is women who have had abortions and regret doing so. For me, to have been <u>forced</u> to have the abortion is more than regret and I find no mere words to describe it. It is different than willingly going in to have an abortion or wanting to get rid of the baby in the womb. But no matter what the circumstance I do regret my abortion!

So if there is a heavenly consolation, it is because of God's mercy, compassion, and love that I know my baby is in heaven. This I know with all my heart. The forgiveness of God for those involved in any way with an abortion is there for the asking with a contrite heart. One must ask to receive. Only through God forgiving can I know that true forgiveness.

That is why when I am in Church and hear a baby's cries, I am not only overwhelmed with emotion, but also overwhelmed with conviction that my baby is in heaven watching everything that God does through me and the Society of the Body of Christ. I find peace knowing that I will live the rest of my life trying to do good.

God creates all of us to become what He intends us to be. No matter what happened in my past, He was going to lead me on through it all, give me the grace to discover the truth and offer me the narrow road to continue to journey on. That was the choice He gave me to make: to follow Him or not.

Through His gifts of courage, fortitude, perseverance, forgiveness and love, I know that no matter what this world tries to do to deter me from following Jesus through Mary, God's Will will be done!

This is why I AM SILENT NO MORE!

Sister Anne-Sophie

IF YOU REGRET YOUR ABORTION OR YOU HAVE BEEN
HURT SOMEHOW BY ABORTION THERE IS HELP!
1-800-395-HELP
www.silentnomoreawareness.org

You can contact Sister Anne Sophie
Society of the Body of Christ
234 Rossiter
Corpus Christi, Texas 78411-1450
361-814-7685
e mail- savesoul@swbell.net

CHECK OUT OUR WEB SITE
WWW.SOCIETYOFTHEBODYOFCHRIST.COM

"THERE IS NO GREATER URGENCY THAN
THE SAVING OF SOULS!"

We are a 501(c) (3) non-profit organization